583
Bus

E6408

D1156477

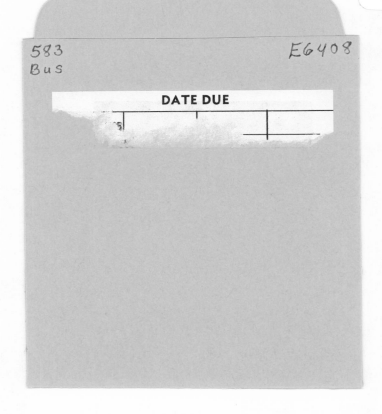

DATE DUE

CACTUS IN THE DESERT

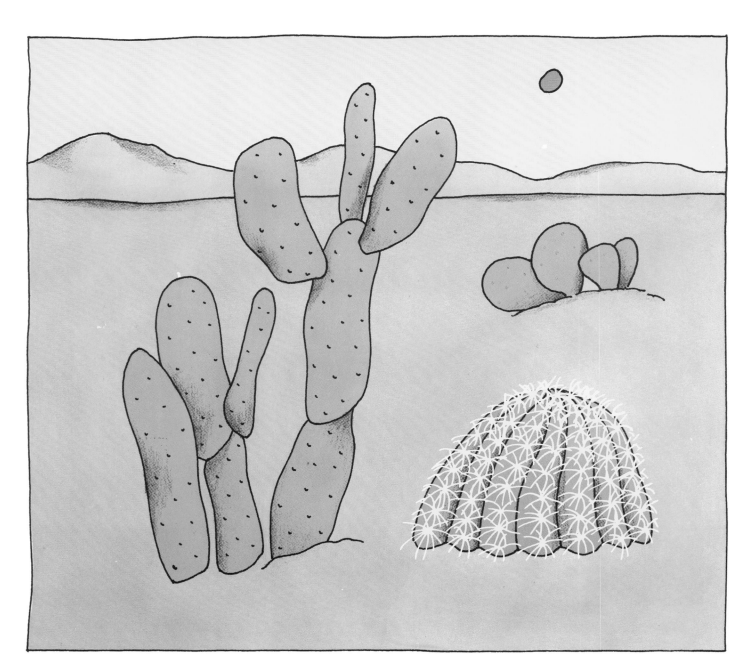

This Is a Let's-Read-and-Find-Out Science Book

CACTUS IN THE DESERT

By Phyllis S. Busch   Illustrated by Harriett Barton

THOMAS Y. CROWELL NEW YORK

OTHER *Let's-Read-and-Find-Out Science Books* YOU WILL ENJOY

Corn Is Maize: The Gift of the Indians by Aliki · *Down Come the Leaves* by Henrietta Bancroft · *How a Seed Grows* by Helene J. Jordan · *Mushrooms and Molds* by Robert Froman · *Plants in Winter* by Joanna Cole · *Roots Are Food Finders* by Franklyn M. Branley · *Seeds by Wind and Water* by Helene J. Jordan · *A Tree Is a Plant* by Clyde Robert Bulla · *Water Plants* by Laurence Pringle · *Where Does Your Garden Grow?* by Augusta Goldin

Let's-Read-and-Find-Out Science Books are edited by Dr. Roma Gans, Professor Emeritus of Childhood Education, Teachers College, Columbia University, and Dr. Franklyn M. Branley, Astronomer Emeritus and former Chairman of The American Museum-Hayden Planetarium. For a complete catalog of *Let's-Read-and-Find-Out Science Books,* write to Thomas Y. Crowell, Department 363, 10 East 53rd Street, New York, New York 10022.

Text copyright © 1979 by Phyllis S. Busch. Illustrations copyright © 1979 by Harriett Barton All rights reserved. Printed in the United States of America. No part of this book may be used or reproduced in any manner whatsoever without written permission except in the case of brief quotations embodied in critical articles and reviews. For information address Thomas Y. Crowell, 10 East 53 Street, New York, N.Y. 10022. Published simultaneously in Canada by Fitzhenry & Whiteside Limited, Toronto.

Library of Congress Cataloging in Publication Data
Busch, Phyllis S. Cactus in the desert. (Let's-read-and-find-out science book)
SUMMARY: Explains how cactus survive in the desert where there is very little water. 1. Cactus—Juvenile literature. 2. Desert flora—Juvenile literature. [1. Cactus. 2. Desert plants] I. Barton, Harriett. II. Title.
QK495.C11B86 (583).47 78-4771 ISBN 0-690-00292-0 ISBN 0-690-01336-1 lib. bdg.
3 4 5 6 7 8 9 10

CACTUS IN THE DESERT

All plants need water. Some plants need a lot of
water. Others need very little.

2

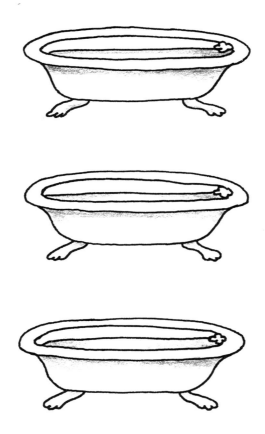

Big trees in woods and forests need a lot of water. They grow where it rains many times in a year. A big tree in a forest may take in 800 quarts (about 760 liters) of water in a day. That's enough to fill two or three bathtubs all the way to the top.

4

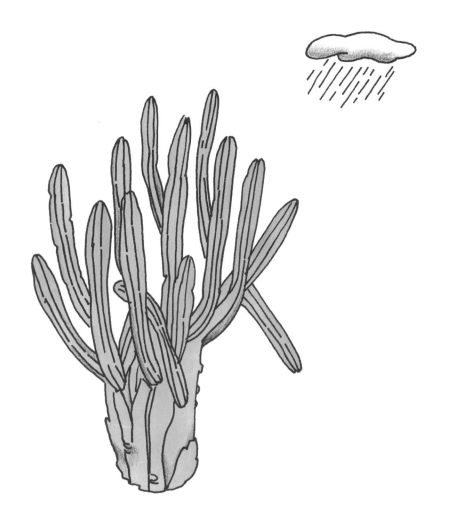

Plants that grow in hot, dry deserts—like cactus
plants—need only a little water. Some of them
grow where it rains only once or twice in a year.

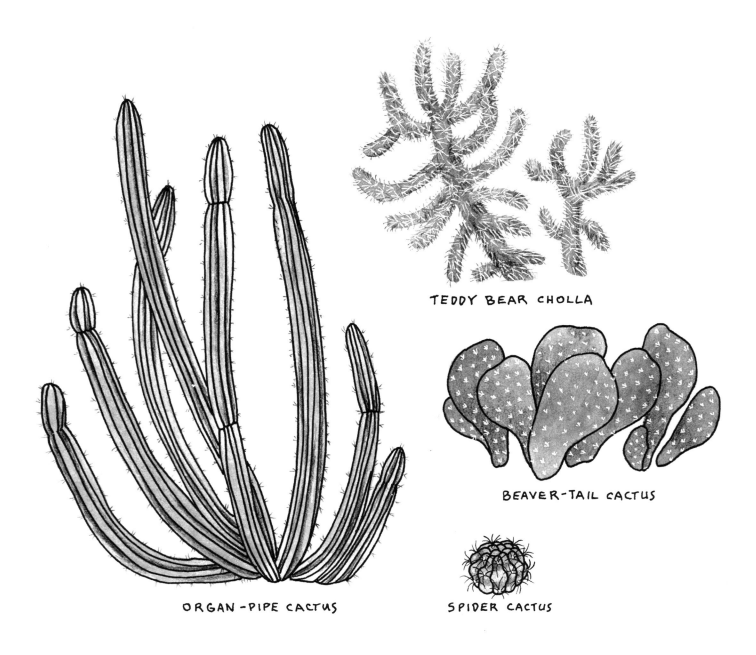

TEDDY BEAR CHOLLA

BEAVER-TAIL CACTUS

ORGAN-PIPE CACTUS

SPIDER CACTUS

Many different kinds of cactus plants live in
deserts. Some are very small. Others are very large.
The pincushion cactus is no bigger than your
thumbnail. Most cactus plants are bigger.

The tallest cactus is called the giant saguaro. It
is also called a tree cactus. A saguaro has a big
stem. It also has many branches that go straight
up. It looks like a telephone pole with branches.

Some saguaros are almost 60 feet tall (about 18
meters). That's higher than ten people standing on
each other's shoulders.

Big plants and little plants get water in the same way. So do plants in the forest and plants in the desert. They get water through their roots.

In leafy plants the water goes from the roots, up the stem, and into the leaves. The leaves use some of the water to make sugar and starch. These are foods for plants.

But most cactus plants have no leaves. They make sugar and starch in their stems.

11

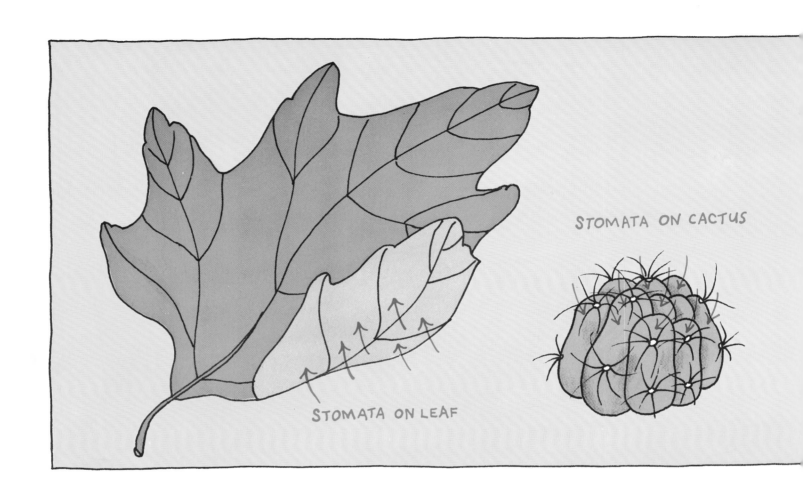

STOMATA ON CACTUS

STOMATA ON LEAF

Plants don't use all the water that they take in. They give off nearly all of it. In most plants the water goes out through small holes on the bottom of the leaves. In a cactus the holes are in the stem.

A single hole is called a stoma. It's a word that means little mouth. Many holes together are called stomata. Whether they are in the leaves or in the stems, you need a microscope to see the stomata because they are so small.

14

When a plant is saving water, the stomata are closed. When it is giving off water, the stomata are open. The water evaporates. It goes into the air.

On a hot day an apple tree gives off a lot of water—as much as 320 quarts (about 300 liters) in a single day. Bigger trees give off even more.

15

A cactus plant also gives off water. But only a little bit. The stem has a very thick, tough skin. There are tiny stomata in the stem. But there are only a few of them, not nearly as many as there are in the leaves of leafy plants. Only a little water can evaporate into the air. On a hot day, a big saguaro cactus loses less than one glass of water.

Water is stored up inside a cactus plant. That is one reason why a cactus plant can live in the desert. It stores water for the long time when there is no rain. Cactus plants store water in their roots and their stems.

LEDGEWOOD SCHOOL
DIST. 131   ROSCOE, IL

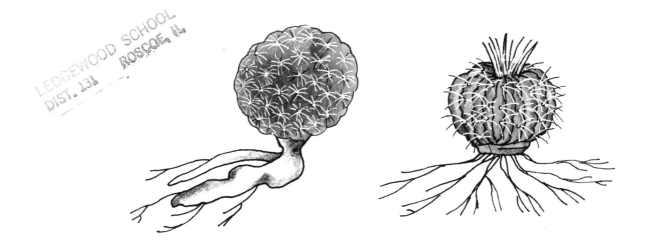

Some cactus plants have fat roots. Others have thin roots, but they have hundreds of them. And they spread out in all directions. The roots from a single plant might cover an area as big as a blanket. Sometimes the area is as big as a tennis court.

When it rains, these small roots collect the water from the whole area that they spread into. Both the fat roots and the thin roots take in a lot of water. The fat roots can store a lot of water, too.

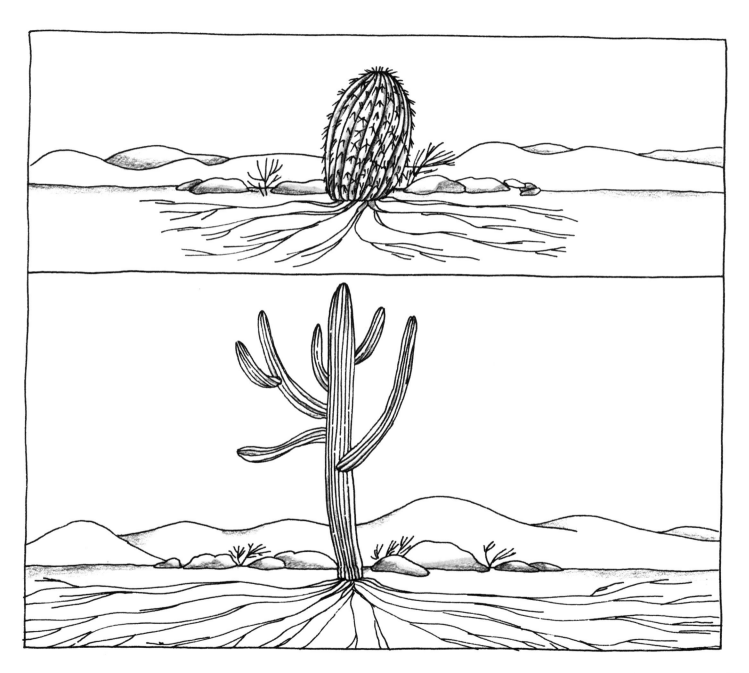

19

Some cactus plants hold a lot of water in their stems. They look like watermelons covered with spines. The spines are as sharp as needles.

One kind is called a barrel cactus because it looks like a little fat barrel. When a cowboy in the desert needs water, he can get it by chewing a piece of this cactus. The watery juice inside is bitter, but the water will keep him alive. That's why people also call this cactus the traveler's friend.

21

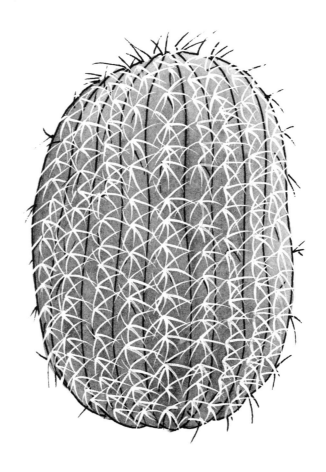

As the barrel cactus uses water, the stem shrivels up a bit.

When it rains, the spiny stem fills up again.

Most cactus plants have spines on their stems.
Some spines are short, straight, and hard. Other
spines are longer, and are curved.

Indians used to break off the curved spines and
use them as fishhooks.

The sharp spines make it hard for most animals
to eat cactus plants. But wood rats eat them.

26

Cattle will eat cactus, too, if the cattle are
hungry enough.

Gila woodpeckers dig holes in cactus plants. Then they make their nests in the holes.

When a cactus is cut, or when a bird digs a hole in it, juice oozes out. But not for long. The juice hardens over the cut, and so stops running out. That's another way that cactus plants save water.

ladyfingers

bunny-ears

peanut

30

pincushion

Cactus plants grow well when they are in a hot dry place. You can find out for yourself. Maybe someone you know raises cactus plants and will give you one. Or you might buy one. These are some kinds you might get: bunny-ears cactus, ladyfingers cactus, peanut cactus, and pincushion cactus.

Indoors a cactus does best in a warm and sunny place. It needs only a little water.

It may grow so slowly that at times you will think it is not growing at all. Yet it may live in your house for years and years. There are cactus plants in the desert that are over 200 years old.

ABOUT THE AUTHOR

Phyllis S. Busch was born in New York City and studied biology at Hunter College. She received a doctoral degree in science education from New York University, and has taught biology and general science from the elementary to the post-graduate level.

Dr. Busch has written many books for children and adults on botanical subjects. The mother of two grown sons, she lives with her husband in Lakeville, Connecticut.

ABOUT THE ILLUSTRATOR

Harriett Barton was born in Picher, Oklahoma, and grew up in nearby Miami. A graduate of the University of Kansas, she presently lives in New York City, where she works as a designer of children's books. She also designs textiles and designs and strings bead necklaces.